# I'm going to be the best superhero ever!

PaRragon

Bath • New York • Singapore • Hong Kong • Cologne • Delhi • Melbourne

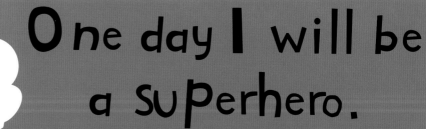

One day I will be a superhero.

Me →

# Most of the time I will look like an ordinary boy.

No one will guess I have superpowers.

I will quickly put on my superhero clothes.

# They will give me special powers.

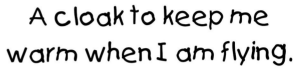

A cloak to keep me warm when I am flying.

Boots with rockets on them to help me fly.

A mask so nobody will recognize me.

A belt that can do tons and tons of clever things.

# Here comes SPEEDYBOY!

**Whoosh!**

# I will help everyone who needs me.

Me rescuing a cat from a tree.

"Meow!"

Me finding a lost soccer ball.

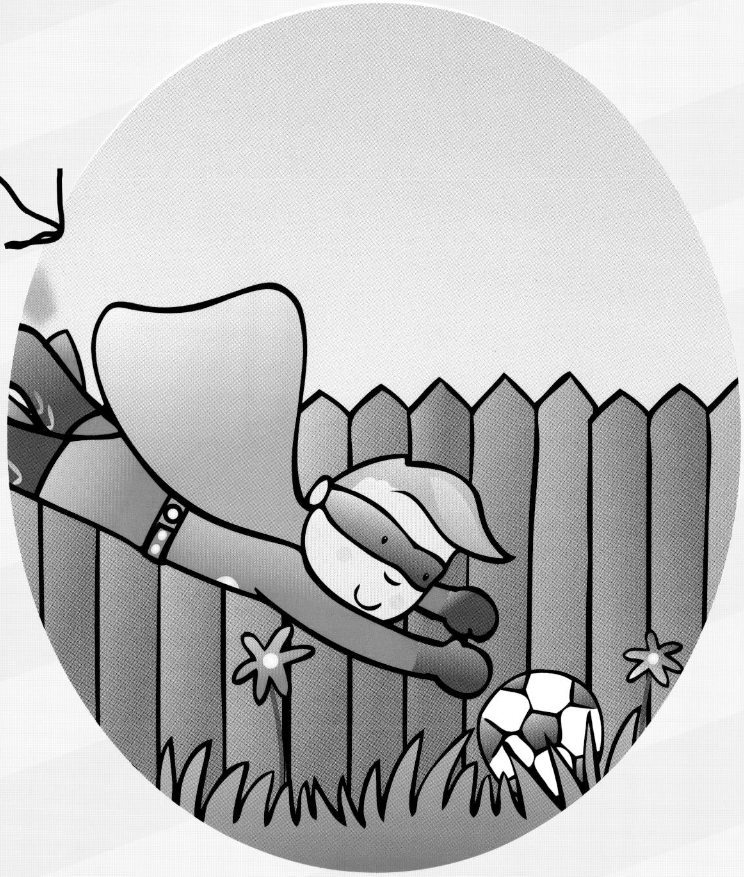

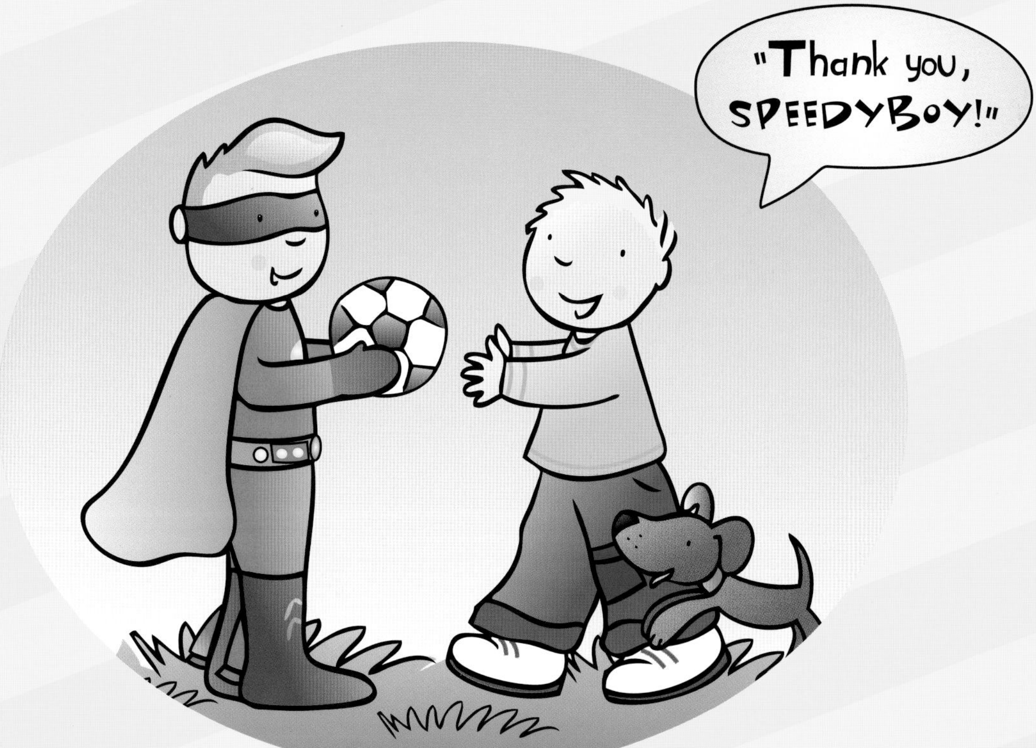

I will be superstrong.

I will eve
be able t
lift a tre

# I will be able to carry people away from danger.

# I will be able to fly even faster than a rocket.

# I will be able to swim underwater like a fish.

# I will be able to blow stronger than the wind.

Rain cloud
blown to
here.
Plants that need
some rain.
"SPEEDYBOY
saved my
plants!"

Sometimes I will meet other superheroes.

# We will have our own superhero club.

# I will be famous all over the world.

Daily News

**SPEEDYBoy** saves us again.

**Who is SPEEDYBoy?**

News Today

Superhero Magazine

**SPEEDYBOY**
Special

SPEEDYBOY
Fan Club

**SPEEDYBOY,
WE LOVE YOU!**

# Everyone will say I am the best superhero ever!

Top superhero →

(but nobody will know it's really me!)

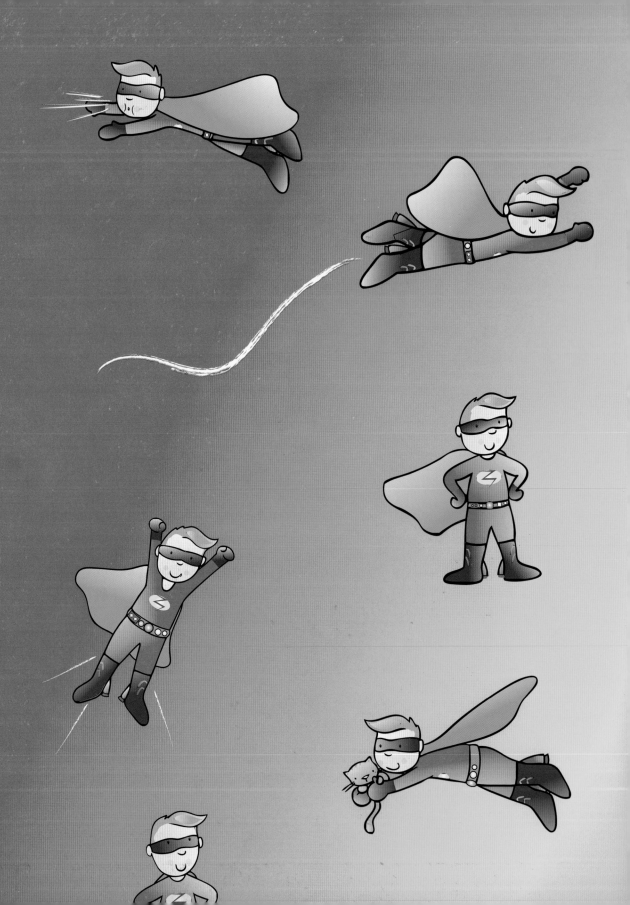